Leaving Home

Sneed B. Collard III   Illustrated by Joan Dunning

For Shelly, May you always feel close to home!

HOUGHTON MIFFLIN COMPANY / BOSTON 2002

Sneed B. Collard III

2002

To the Lourie family,
who helped make leaving home a spectacular adventure.
Love, Sneed III

For my daughter, Suzanne, my first-born,
who is getting ready to leave home as I illustrate this book.
May she take wing and savor flight.
—J. D.

www.houghtonmifflinbooks.com

The text of this book is set in Goudy and Frutiger.
The illustrations are watercolors.

Library of Congress Cataloging-in-Publication Data

Collard, Sneed B.
Leaving home / by Sneed B. Collard ; illustrated by Joan Dunning.
p. cm.
Summary: Surveys the behavior of various young animals and describes how
they eventually grow old enough to leave their parents.
ISBN 0-618-11454-8
1. Animal behavior—Juvenile literature. [1. Animals—Infancy. 2. Animals—
Habits and behavior.] I. Dunning, Joan, 1948–   II. Title.

QL751.5 .C574 2002
591.5—dc21   2001039252

Printed in Singapore
TWP 10 9 8 7 6 5 4 3 2 1

Sooner or later, we all leave home.

Some of us walk.

Reaching two to three hundred pounds, jaguars are America's largest cats. But they don't start out that way. Jaguars weigh only a couple of pounds at birth and drink mother's milk for their first six months of life. As they grow in size and strength, they begin hunting with mom and learning other skills they need to survive. Finally, when they are between one and two years old, they leave their mother's side for good and seek out their own individual territories.

Some of us crawl.

Most crabs live in the ocean, but the Jamaican bromeliad crab starts life in a small pool of water trapped in a bromeliad plant. Mother brings food to the baby crabs, protects them from hungry lizards and spiders, and clears dead leaves from the pool. When a young crab is six months to a year old, it finally skitters away to look for its own plant pool paradise.

Some of us fly.

Like most other birds of prey, rough-legged hawk parents feed their ravenous chicks for several months after they hatch. The downy youngsters quickly reach adult size and grow their flying feathers. They hop and flap, testing their skills, then make their first awkward flights. It's none too soon. Within weeks, the young birds will take off to warmer wintering grounds—the first of many migrations they'll make during their lifetimes.

And some of us swim.

Many sharks bear live babies that swim free as soon as they're born. However, the Port Jackson shark lays eggs in egg cases that the mother wedges in between rocks. A large yolk sac inside the egg case provides food for each youngster as it grows and looks more and more like a shark. After nine to twelve months, the baby shark finally wriggles from its egg-case cocoon. Then it swims away to begin its life hunting sea urchins and shellfish.

Currents carry some of us.

Most baby corals hatch from eggs that have been released into the sea by their parents. At this stage in life, they are called *larvae*—tiny animals that look more like space aliens than corals. As larvae, the young corals float on ocean currents that can carry them dozens, or even hundreds, of miles. After one or two weeks, the coral larvae sink to the bottom, attach themselves to a reef, and—like caterpillars changing into butterflies—metamorphose into tiny versions of their parents.

And so do the winds.

When they're ready to leave home, many spiders rely not on their legs, but on the wind. They climb to the top of a log or other high place and release long, light strands of silk. With luck, breezes catch these silky "balloons" and tug the spiders into the sky. Most ballooning flights are short, but some can last for days and carry the spiders to heights of 18,000 feet before they touch down in new scampering grounds.

We hitchhike,

A young remora's biggest job is to find a host to swim around with. The host can be another fish, a sea turtle, whale, or shark. When it grows tired of swimming, the remora sticks to its host, using the special suction cup on its head. When it spots some food, the remora detaches itself, gulps down a meal, and then latches back onto its host. Some remoras pay for their rides by picking off harmful parasites from the host's skin, mouth, and gills.

Hop,

Under the right conditions, an adult female wild rabbit can give birth to as many as forty-five babies a year. The babies are born blind and helpless, but are weaned after only four or five weeks. The young males are forced from the rabbit colony to look for their own territories. Young female rabbits "hop" closer to home, but they still have to compete for good grazing areas and burrows.

And glide.

Flying lizards—also called "flying dragons"—live in the tall rain forests of Southeast Asia. The young hatch from eggs on the ground and climb into the trees to hunt insects. The lizards are born with especially long ribs webbed with skin. To reach other trees, the lizards spread these skin-covered "wings" and glide as far as thirty feet to another tree trunk or branch. The only time flying dragons return to the ground is to lay eggs for a new batch of lizard acrobats.

We can leave home by ourselves.

Weighing up to fifty pounds, wolverines search vast northern mountain ranges for animal carcasses to feed on. A mother wolverine gives birth to one, two, or three kits. They stay with her for a year or two, learning to find carcasses, browse on berries, and dig through snow to catch marmots. Then, one by one, the young wolverines leave to establish their own territories, alone in the wild north.

And also in large groups.

Wildebeests, or gnus, live in a traveling metropolis. More than one million migrate through the plains of East Africa searching for grass to eat. All the females give birth at about the same time. So many newborns arrive at once that hyenas and other predators are overwhelmed and have time to eat only a few of the gnu babies. Several days later, the surviving youngsters are ready to join the rest of the herd as it continues its remarkable roving lifestyle.

A few of us know where we're going.

Each winter, mother gray whales give birth to their calves in warm lagoons along the Pacific coast of Mexico. The calves nurse for several weeks. In spring, they accompany their mothers on a 7,000-mile journey to northern coastal feeding grounds. No one is sure how, but the whales know exactly where they are going and often show up at the same feeding grounds year after year. In the fall, the young whales find their way back to Mexico completely on their own.

Most others only guess.

Unlike whales, Gila monsters and most other animals are born without knowing exactly where they should go. But most animal babies do have instincts to guide them. Once they hatch or are born, their instincts may tell them to follow certain smells, seek out water, or find holes to live in. Many young animals make mistakes and die or are eaten, but the fortunate ones find the food, water, and shelter they need to survive.

Some of us leave when we're young.

Many salamanders lay their eggs in water and, like frogs, leave them to hatch and develop on their own. The red-backed salamander, though, lays her eggs in rotting logs or under rocks. Mom wraps herself around the eggs, protecting them until they hatch. Afterward, the young stay with her for only a week or two before searching out new homes rich with insects, worms, millipedes, and spiders to eat.

And others, later on.

Newborn African elephant babies weigh up to 250 pounds, but that doesn't mean they're ready to leave home. Young African elephants live in family groups composed of several adult females. The babies depend on these families to protect them, feed them, and teach them survival skills. After three to five years, the young males, or bulls, gradually break away from the family to live with other bulls. Female elephants may remain in the family for many more years and may even replace older females when they leave or die.

We can travel across oceans,

After being raised by its parents, a yearling wandering albatross heads out to sea and may not set foot on land again for five to ten years. The bird's ten-foot wings carry it thousands of miles across oceans as it hunts squid, fish, and cuttlefish to eat. In just nine weeks, biologists tracked one albatross almost 20,000 miles! The birds rest by floating on the ocean surface and only return to land to mate and raise their chicks.

Over tall mountains,

During the dry season, hundreds of different kinds of Costa Rican butterflies leave the coastal lowland forests. They flutter inland, up tropical valleys until they reach wetter forests high in the mountains. Many cross the continental divide, and here they feed on rotting fruits and the nectar of flowers. Many also mate, lay eggs, and die. Their eggs hatch into caterpillars, metamorphose into butterflies, and return over the mountains to the lowland forests the following spring.

Or just down the street.

After being raised by mom for four to six weeks, young European hedgehogs—or hoglets—venture out on their own. Unlike many other mammals, hedgehogs don't often wander far. They simply roam a half-mile or mile every night looking for slugs, worms, and beetles to eat. By dawn, they settle down in any cozy nest site they come across. In England, the hedgehogs make a good living hunting in people's backyard shrubs and leaf piles. Many people welcome them by setting out dishes of water and canned dog food.

When we leave, it's exciting . . .

Thick-billed murres raise their chicks on dizzying cliffs above the ocean. When a chick is about twenty days old, its father leads it to the cliff edge, where it leaps. The chick can't fly, but it glides down to the water with its parent and other adult murres close behind. Under their parents' watchful eyes, the chicks paddle out to sea, swimming as far as 600 miles to their wintering grounds before they can fly and hunt for themselves.

And a little bit sad.

Bear mothers invest a lot of time and energy in their young. They feed them, teach them, and protect them from enemies. It's no wonder many youngsters are reluctant to leave mom's side. Eventually, though, the mother bear quits being nice to her youngsters. She may even drive them away so they will live on their own—and so she can mate and raise a new set of cubs.

We find new companions,

Young North American garter snakes spend their first winter hibernating in places scientists still haven't discovered. But for their second winter, the young snakes often join thousands of adult garter snakes. They gather in large underground caves, forming huge masses that look like giant balls of yarn. The snakes huddle together for up to eight months. Then they emerge to mate, hunt, and bear a new crop of garter snake babies.

And become who we're meant to be.

Frogs are some of the millions of animals that start out looking very different from their parents. Most frogs begin life as tadpoles, swimming around in pools, ponds, or streams. At this stage, it's hard to tell exactly what they'll turn into. Only when the tadpoles develop legs and lose their tails do we know what kinds of frogs they are—and the kinds of lives they will lead.

But no matter who we are . . .

Five species of rhinoceroses live across Africa and Asia. Two species, the Indian and white rhinos, are the world's largest land mammals besides elephants. Like elephants, rhinos reproduce slowly, giving birth to a baby every two to three years. A young rhino often stays with its mom until the next baby is born. After that, the rhinos may live in small herds, but most set out on solitary lives, finding their own territories to live and graze in.

Or what we look like . . .

Chambered nautiluses live in deep waters around tropical coral reefs. The female nautilus lays its eggs on the ocean floor. When the babies hatch, their shells are already about an inch long. As the babies explore their deep-water worlds, their shells help protect them from predators. The shells also act as floats, carrying them up to shallower waters every night so they can hunt lobsters and hermit crabs for food.

We all leave home. A few of us even . . .

find our way back.

After they hatch and get their feathers, North American barn swallows migrate to Central and South America for the winter. The following spring, they—and many other birds—return to the area where they were born to build their own nests and raise their young.